GarethGates
Right From The Start
Written by Gareth Gates
with Siân Solanas

I'd like to thank Mum and Dad for all the love and support they've given me all my life. I wouldn't be where I am now without the time and the effort that they've invested in me; their continual encouragement has been invaluable.

Also my three sisters Nicola, Charlotte and Jessica, and my foster brother James. Firstly, I'd like to thank you Nicola for always being there, you're my best friend and you'll always be. James – all I'll say is: be good. Charlotte and Jessica – now you've got some more to read, so Dad will be pleased.

To the whole of the family – **'John'**.

First published in Great Britain in 2002 by **Virgin Books Ltd**, Thames Wharf Studios, Rainville Road, London W6 9HA.

Copyright ©**19 Merchandising Limited** 2002
Management: **Simon Fuller at 19 Management**
The right of GarethGates to be identified as the Author of this Work has been asserted by him in accordance with the Copyright, Designs and Patents Act, 1988.

A catalogue record for this book is available from the British Library. ISBN 1 85227 914 1
Printed and bound in Great Britain by **Butler & Tanner**
Photographs: **Terry McGough**: cover, 5, 6–7, 32–33, 40–41, 50–51, 56–57, 61, 80; **Nazirin**: inside cover, 35, 36, 39 (bottom right), 42–43, 43 (bottom right), 44, 45, 47, 48, 49, 53, 54, 62, 63, 64–65, 65, 68, 70, 71, 72–73, 74, 75, 76, 78, 79; **Jeff Spicer**: 3, 25 (bottom right, top right), 30–31, 42 (top left), 64 (left), 66–67; **Fremantle Media Enterprises**: 8, 9, 23, 25 (top left, middle right, bottom right), 26, 27, 28, 29; **Paul & Wendy Gates**: 10, 12, 14–15, 17, 18, 19, 20, 25 (middle left); **Camilla Howarth**: 39 (top left, middle left, bottom left, top centre, top right, middle right); **Nicol Nodland**: 58, 59.

Design by **EgelnickandWebb**.com

Contents

Dear readers,

It's been a frantic few months. Since the **Pop Idol** final my feet have hardly touched the ground. I've released two massive singles, recorded my album, played to enormous crowds during the whole summer and have been mobbed everywhere I've been – and that is a lot of places.

Welcome to my story so far. As you know, I'm only eighteen, so this could never be called a proper autobiography. This is my life, from my perspective, from the moment that I was born, through my head choirboy days, to my life as a number one pop star.

Some have called me 'an overnight success'. Once you read this book, you'll see not only how hard I worked to fulfil my dream, but you'll see the achievements I made before I appeared on **Pop Idol** – achievements I'm proud of for myself and some that have helped others.

For the first time, in detail, I can reveal how I cope with the fame, the pressure, the attention ... and the girls. Read how I've tried to conquer my stammer, without letting it get in the way of what I've wanted to do all my life – music.

I would like to give a special thank you to Simon Fuller and all the team at 19 Management and equally Simon Cowell and all at BMG Records. You've put my dream into reality.

I'd like to thank my friends, my family who've watched all this happen and all the teachers who've helped me make the most of what I'm good at. You've all stuck by me and for that I'm eternally grateful.

With love,

Gareth x

MY STORY
Chapter 1

'I went in and it took me **ages** to **introduce myself**'

'There were masses of people at the **Pop Idol** audition in Manchester, July 2001. I walked into the waiting room and people were practising their scales, the toilets were full of people standing in front of the mirrors, checking themselves out, and everyone was nervous. I sat there, waiting my turn. I wasn't really talking to anyone, I was listening to what everyone was saying, and all they were talking about was this nasty guy who was part of the judging panel in the audition room. And from what I could gather, he was not being very polite to people he felt lacked talent ... to say the least, and judging by the people coming out of there, he didn't think there was much talent on offer that afternoon! Some people walked out of the auditions crying, some people were refusing to go into the auditions because they were so worried about what he might say to them. I didn't want to be put off, I knew I was there to do my best, so I tried not to listen to what everyone else was saying and concentrate on my performance.

I had other things to worry about – I had to announce my name in front of strangers and, for someone with a stammer, that's the most difficult thing to do. I could sing and I looked all right, but I was sure they wanted a pop star – and pop stars don't have stammers.

I went in and it took me ages to introduce myself: about twenty seconds to come out with the words "Gareth Gates". I was frozen, completely eaten up with nerves. The judges were patient and they let me take my time. The difficult part was over, the nerves died down and I sang the song I had rehearsed over and over: Westlife's "Flying Without Wings". The people in the room sat in stunned silence: after they'd seen that I wasn't able to speak properly, they were shocked to hear that I could sing with no stammer at all. I for one felt relieved that I'd got through this ordeal.

Each of the judges was complimentary – they liked my voice, they thought I looked the part, they knew I had a stammer ... I was dreading what they were going to say.

I recognised Pete Waterman and Dr Fox, and Nicki Chapman I'd seen as a judge on **Popstars**. But there was one man who I presumed everyone had been talking about beforehand, because I didn't recognise him at all. He looked at me and said, calmly, "You're going to London. Well done." YES!

I was made up, overjoyed. I rushed out of the audition room and hugged my sister Nicola, who was there auditioning too. "I'm going to London!" I shouted.

For someone who almost didn't get the application form in time, I was thrilled that I was part of what became the biggest TV talent show ever, a programme which attracted an audience of over thirteen million viewers. Little did I know, although I really hoped, that through the programme I'd get a management contract and a record deal with two of the top players in the music industry ... a first single that went to number one for four weeks and a place in the **Guinness Book of Records**. Both Simon Fuller, the man who created **Pop Idol** and the man who was to be known throughout the country as the new Mr Nasty, Simon Cowell, had given me the opportunity to do what I had always wanted.

'I had a **stammer** from the **moment** I tried to speak'

'My first memory is of the flat we had in Bradford. I must have been about two. I was stood outside my bedroom door, looking left into the kitchen through the window and I remember it being very bright outside. I had a robot toy, which you put cards into make it speak. I remember it said, "A is for apple", "B is for banana" in an American accent. The robot was on the floor in front of me but the light got my attention.

I was born Gareth Paul Gates in St Luke's Hospital, Bradford, on 12 July 1984, to Paul and Wendy Gates. I weighed 6lb 12oz and my mum says I had big feet and ... yes, spiky hair, both of which I still have. My mum says I was a happy baby, I didn't cry too much and was well behaved. I was walking by the time I was ten months old, which was early; my first tooth came at fourteen months, which was late.

My dad worked in engineering for many years, but the long hours and the responsibility of the job eventually put a strain on our family life. He decided to get a simpler job with less hours: he got a job as a postman. My mum's a foster carer. I've got a sister, Nicola, who's ten and a half months younger than me. We're very close and we used to sing together. Then there's Charlotte who is eleven and Jessica who's eight. I get on really well with all of them.

I was seven when my mum started fostering, so soon I was used to seeing little children coming in and out of the house. I never had any worries about it. We all had a big family meeting beforehand and we went through every detail, so we were always happy about it. My mum wanted to help people and I come from that sort of family.

We first started looking after my cousin James, who's two years younger than me, when I was seven. He's been with us so long now he's like my brother, and it was good to have another boy in the house so that we could play football. About three years ago, my mum got into link foster caring. We have the children from when they leave their parents to when they go back or go to a new home. The link foster carer has the children in the in-between stage, which can be from one day to three years. We'd often have two children at a time, siblings, so they could stay together until they found a permanent home. It's never been a problem, my mum and dad are great at looking after them, so the only hard thing is to let go of them.

As a child I had an active imagination. When I went to the pictures to see the film **Superman**, I immediately demanded the whole of my bedroom to be decked out in Superman wallpaper. My mum and dad spent a fortune on the wallpaper, they also got me a Superman carpet, Superman duvet cover, pillowcases, curtains and lampshade – everything. On the first night it was finished, I was put to bed, but I ran out straight afterwards and got into my mum and dad's bed, because it scared me so much! The wallpaper was so dark, and then there was Superman on the wall, up in the sky, flying at me with his arm pointed out. I was terrified. After a week I was fine; I got used to it in the end.

The only other memory I have from that flat, before we moved into a larger house in another part of Bradford, was being in the living room with my sister. Mum and Dad were sitting on the sofa; Nicola and me were messing about, pretending to eat sweets. You put your tongue in your cheek and you

'But Mrs Gates, have you heard your son sing?'

pretend you're chewing. We were pleading with our parents to give us a sweet, real or otherwise, so they pretended to give us one and we shouted, "Oh, that's so nice!" and carried on chewing. We kept ourselves amused.

Strangely, there wasn't a lot of music in the house when I was growing up. My Dad liked UB40. He's from Birmingham and so are they, so we listened to them, and he loved Bob Marley too. Neither of my parents could sing, and I never sang until I was eight – but when I did …

I had a stammer from the moment I tried to put sentences together, which my parents recognised because my dad had a stammer up until he was eighteen, which he grew out of (my sister Charlotte has one too; sometimes it's hereditary). My stammer

got worse over the years and at five I was referred to a speech therapist, but this didn't really help me. My stammer would make me completely unable to say a sentence properly, but I didn't want this ever to get in the way of what I wanted to do.

When I was five, my mum took me to an audition to play one of the King's sons in the musical **The King and I**, which was being put on at the Alhambra Theatre in Bradford. The auditions took a long time, and after the first round I was made to sit and wait. My mum left me for a while, telling me to sit next to and stay with two older girls and behave. But when the director, Steve Dexter, told these two girls that they hadn't gone through to the next round of auditions, I – thinking I had to do as they did – left the room as well.

My mum confronted me outside.

"Were you sent out?" she asked. "Never mind, son."

"No," I said, "I wasn't sent out. I followed the girls."

"Why did you come out?"

"The girls I was with came out."

"You get yourself back in there!" she said, and hurried me back.

I went back in and got through each round of the auditions. I knew that Steve Dexter had taken a shine to me, he said I'd be a star one day – I was only five!

I played the youngest child of the King because I was the smallest, and looked cute and slightly bemused by the whole thing. There was a scene when each of the children greet the dad and I'm so small I'm forgotten about, so I have to tug at his trousers and make myself known. I had the part which made everyone laugh. I admit now that I didn't know I was doing, but it was a lot of fun. I knew from then – perhaps even before then – that I wanted to perform, in some way or another.

The next time I got on stage was three years later. My first school was putting on a performance of **Joseph and his Amazing Technicolor Dreamcoat**. I went to the auditions for a laugh, because my mates were doing it, and I thought I might get the part of one of Joseph's brothers.

We knew the main song from the musical, "Any Dream Will Do", because it had been a hit record by Jason Donovan and it was a school favourite. The teacher asked me to sing it, the first time I had ever sung in public – in truth, the first time I had sung at all. I stood there, opened my mouth to sing and everyone was stunned. I had a voice.

Of course, it was a shock to everyone and me because I couldn't speak properly, but the main thing was that I had a really good voice – it was clean and pure. I came home and told my parents I was sure to be one of the brothers. The next day I came home and told Mum I was Joseph. A little taken aback, she went into school to ask why the role had changed and my teacher said, "But Mrs Gates, have you heard your son sing?"

"No ..." she said.

"He's got the most incredible voice!"

My mum came back home, very excited, and told me to sing to her but I refused, saying that she had to wait for the performance – I was cheeky like that. I knew I could keep my parents waiting and the surprise would be even bigger.

A girl called Helen had gone for the part of Joseph and really wanted it, so we shared the role. I was Joseph for the first half and she was Joseph for the second – in the middle of the show she came on stage and she took my coat, and I walked off. The musical doesn't have lines, it's all sung, so it was OK for me to be in it. I loved it.

This was the start of Gareth Gates the singer ... and the girls got interested. There's a wicked song in the play which goes, "I was wandering along the banks of the river ..." where the Pharaoh's telling Joseph about his dream. I had a crush on the girl who played the Pharaoh; she had ginger hair ... I thought she was great. I was a bit fickle when I was little: a couple of days later I fell in love with someone else! I had a different girlfriend every week; I've always been popular with girls but now I was even more popular.

By this time I had started playing guitar at the school. The guitar teacher, Mr Jones, thought I was good; when I left to go to

'I was always quite **naughty ...'**

secondary school, he asked me if I wanted to have private guitar lessons. He was cool, he played classical guitar and electric guitar for when he played rock, but I learnt purely classical. Eventually I got to grade eight classical guitar, mainly because I practised for an hour a day, almost every day. I studied hard at everything as a child. I knew I had to put my all into things, especially because I never wanted my stammer to get in the way. My school reports were great: there were merit awards stuck everywhere. I wasn't the brightest in the class but I was the person who worked hard. People who are really bright don't have to do so much work, they have it all in their heads, but I have to concentrate extra hard – I'm the one who's never finished early in an exam, I'm still on question one when the teacher announces there's five minutes left. In middle school I wasn't the best at reading and spelling, but after that I started to work hard and I was top of my class.

I used to like every class, music – even maths, I love maths. I wanted to do maths A level but I had to choose between that and music, because the schedules clashed.

I wasn't just a swot, a goody-goody. Me and my mates used to do some funny stuff which was quite bad looking back. When it was snowing, Lee (who was my best mate) and I, and other friends, used to play up a bit. We'd get my foster brother, James, to knock on people's doors and then make him run back and hide behind a wall. When the person opened the door, we'd jump up from behind the wall, throw snowballs at him and try to get them into his hallway.

There was a really grumpy old man who lived down the road. James would knock on the front door, the man would open the door and James would say something really rude to him and run away, just because we told him too. The things he said were so rude, I couldn't tell you here, they were so bad and I'm quite ashamed of myself for making him do that. Sorry James.

Every night, me and my friends would play out till late, in our street. My mum and dad's second house was just outside Bradford town, so there was lots of space, but you'd still be about ten minutes away from everywhere. Bradford is a small place compared to Manchester or London, and everything's nearby.

I miss all that now, I wish I could be eight again, we were always kicking a football around. Lee and I would often run in to get our dads out for football so it would be children against the dads. We were good at football. Our street was called Lillian Street and we used to play teams from other streets and have local tournaments. The main game would always be between the best two teams in the area, obviously, and it was Lillian Street versus Fenby Avenue. We were very hard to beat and we always ended up playing them – we lost a few times but it was always close. Those children were eighteen and we were eleven, so we were really good. If I hadn't got into music at eight I would have been a footballer.

When I started middle school at Lowerfields, they knew I had a good voice, so I got to sing a lot of the solo parts in

'The choirmaster said I had one of **the best** voices he'd heard'

the school concerts. It was at this school a teacher, who knew the choirmaster Alan Horsey, advised me to go for an audition for the Bradford Cathedral choir; he said I had a fantastic voice. My mum rang Alan up.

"Bring Gareth down and I'll listen to him," he said.

I went along, sang and I was taken as a choirboy aged nine straight away. Alan said I had one of the best voices he'd heard at a first audition.

The cathedral is where it all started. Singing with that type of choir gives you the best grounding for your voice you can have. For five years I was there all the time – I practised on Monday, Thursday and Saturday and sang on Sunday. We also went on tour, to Germany, Guernsey, the New Forest ... After I'd been there for two years, at eleven, I was made head choirboy and sang lots of solos in the cathedral. My family thought I was the new Aled Jones! Because I was singing all the time, I got used to performing in front of large audiences and this made up my mind: I wanted to be an opera singer. I hadn't discovered pop music; it was purely classical. I also became less and less nervous about performing, which meant that years later, when I was singing live every week on **Pop Idol** in front of millions of viewers, I had very few nerves at all. I especially want to thank Alan Horsey, the choirmaster. He was the first one who taught me everything about singing and he was the person who gave me opportunities. I took the Associated Board grades in singing and reached grade eight by the time I was sixteen.

I've been going to the Abundant Life Centre in Bradford with all the family since

most weeks and I was involved with the youth band, which had rehearsals Friday night and a meeting on Saturday night.

Sometimes I think I'm busy now, but when I was younger I was out every evening and at weekends, I was at church all the time unless I had a lot of school work or exams. It was manic; my mum and dad would tell me to pace everything, but they always encouraged me if I wanted to do something. A typical day would be spent at college full time, from 8.30 a.m., finished at 3.30 p.m. I'd come home, go straight to my guitar lesson, come back and have something to eat then go to church for 6 p.m. to do the youth band rehearsal,

'I learnt about **harmonies** from **the church**'

I was five. It was at church that I really got into playing electric guitar and learning how to structure pop songs. It's not a typical church with age-old hymns and people mouthing the words.

The church is amazing. There are services on Sunday morning, Sunday evening and Wednesday night. The congregation is about 1,500 and it's growing all the time. Every meeting is full of modern songs sung in a pop style with a band (the Worship Team) and everyone sings. It feels more like a concert than a service sometimes, but there's a sermon too. The Worship Team sings the songs on stage and I was part of that from thirteen. Members of the Worship Team write the songs to sing and that's partly how I learnt about up-tempo pop songs and how to write them. I was singing

then the main band rehearsal at 7.30 p.m. I'd be there till about eleven at night; once I was home, I did any homework I had for the next day.

I made some good friends at the church, Elan and Heather, who I still see. I used to hang out with my sister Nicola – I'd call her my best friend – we've always been so close.

I have a joke with Zoë Birkett from **Pop Idol**, she calls me the "Harmony King" because when someone's singing a tune, I can instantly put a harmony to it. I learnt all that from the church – while I was there I had to teach the choir harmony parts: soprano, alto, tenor and bass.

It was around then that I started to understand the church and the Bible – we believe that if you have a talent you should

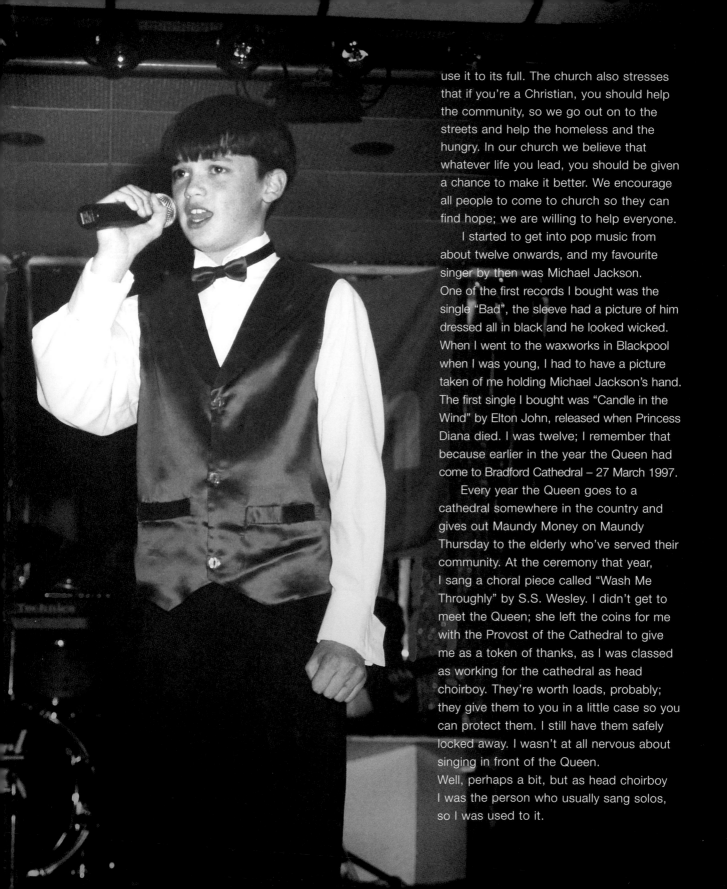

use it to its full. The church also stresses that if you're a Christian, you should help the community, so we go out on to the streets and help the homeless and the hungry. In our church we believe that whatever life you lead, you should be given a chance to make it better. We encourage all people to come to church so they can find hope; we are willing to help everyone.

I started to get into pop music from about twelve onwards, and my favourite singer by then was Michael Jackson. One of the first records I bought was the single "Bad", the sleeve had a picture of him dressed all in black and he looked wicked. When I went to the waxworks in Blackpool when I was young, I had to have a picture taken of me holding Michael Jackson's hand. The first single I bought was "Candle in the Wind" by Elton John, released when Princess Diana died. I was twelve; I remember that because earlier in the year the Queen had come to Bradford Cathedral – 27 March 1997.

Every year the Queen goes to a cathedral somewhere in the country and gives out Maundy Money on Maundy Thursday to the elderly who've served their community. At the ceremony that year, I sang a choral piece called "Wash Me Throughly" by S.S. Wesley. I didn't get to meet the Queen; she left the coins for me with the Provost of the Cathedral to give me as a token of thanks, as I was classed as working for the cathedral as head choirboy. They're worth loads, probably; they give them to you in a little case so you can protect them. I still have them safely locked away. I wasn't at all nervous about singing in front of the Queen.
Well, perhaps a bit, but as head choirboy I was the person who usually sang solos, so I was used to it.

'I sang in front of the **Queen** – I wasn't at all nervous'

I was in charge of the choir; what was worse than singing was having to tell lads who were older than me what to do, because I was twelve and some of them were fifteen. I'd say, "Don't mess around in the choir stalls!" to try to keep everyone in order but it took me a couple of months to be able to do that.

It also took me a while to be comfortable in what I was wearing, the full choirboy outfit which looked like a big dress. One of the first Sundays I was singing at the cathedral, my mates came down and as I walked down the aisle at the start of the service, they stood watching me. I could feel their eyes on me, so I looked round and they were laughing their heads off. I mouthed "Sorry" because I felt so silly and was immediately told to stand back in line.

My sister was also a member of the cathedral choir and I used to have to tell her off too if she messed about and didn't concentrate.

"You're not telling me what to do!" she'd shout back.

"It's my choir," I'd reply, "so don't mess me about."

"I'll tell Mum you shouted at me ..." She'd tell Mum and Mum would say that yes, I was in charge of the choir and I was right. Nicola hated that.

I used to sing outside church and the cathedral, too. There were talent competitions held at a caravan park we used to go to in the summer, on the east coast. When I was young, I didn't sing the type of music that was suited to the competitions, really. I used to sing Andrew Lloyd Webber's "Love Changes Everything" while everyone else would be singing pure pop, but I had a

'I **lived** through my music because I couldn't speak well'

place in the national finals almost every year.

When I was fourteen, I was at the talent show in the caravan park, singing "I Will Always Love You" by Whitney Houston. When I got to the high notes, I could tell that things weren't quite right. My voice was breaking.

I had to come early from one holiday because I had to do a concert in St George's Hall, a concert hall in Bradford. It was Mendelssohn's **Elijah** and I had a major solo to do. On the day of the show, I was rehearsing my piece where I had to reach a high note, and it was very difficult. It was just below high C, and in the end I had to change the way I sang this note because it was so difficult – before that, I could reach high C and above. On the night, I stood up and sang, knowing it was

going to be tough. When it came to the note I just went for it ... and it worked! The note was perfect. But I'd never be able to reach it ever again and it took a lot to get it out of me!

I worked on my voice while my voice was breaking, to help me get to my lower voice. Some singing coaches don't advise it, but I sang while it was deepening and I think it helped me feel comfortable with my lower range.

I stepped down from my role as head choirboy and began to sing alto, then tenor. I also began to sing with my sister in the holiday park competitions; we did duets like "All I Ask of You" from **Phantom of the Opera**. We did a lot: we went on a TV show called **Talent for Tomorrow**, hosted by Lisa Riley. We were also one of the acts chosen to represent Yorkshire TV in a national talent competition; the other act was a guy who played the cornet. We competed against finalists from Granada TV, Tyne Tees and so on, and got quite far.

I'd been on TV on my own before, on **Michael Barrymore's My Kind of People** in the Meadowhall Centre in Sheffield in 1995, just before I sang for the Queen. I signed my very first autograph when I left the stage.

I sang "Pie Jesu" from Andrew Lloyd Webber's **Requiem** on the Yorkshire TV news programme **Tonight**. My mum and I wrote them a letter to say who I was, that the last performance I'd done had been singing for the Queen, and could I sing on the programme? They rang back and said they'd love to have me on – I was becoming well-known locally. I still had guitar and singing lessons and was intent on becoming an opera singer. I entered **Steps to the Stars**, another talent contest hosted by Claire and H from Steps.I got thousands of votes from the viewers and I got through to the final. Little did I know that the next year I'd be getting millions of votes from TV viewers.

Again, nerves didn't come into it. When I was singing I was confident, I lived through my singing voice and my music because I couldn't speak well. The singing was the easy part. The older I got, the worse my stammer became and I felt unable to control that side of things. I'd had no more therapy on my speaking voice since I was five but I was determined to do my best and not let it get me down. Perhaps at some of the caravan park sites I was nervous, but nothing much makes me nervous now. Nights of live singing in **Pop Idol**? A walk in the park! Kind of.

At school, I was becoming a bit of a star. Everyone knew me because of my music, they'd seen me on TV and at school concerts. From not singing at all until I was eight, I sang every day of my life from then on, I did family weddings and when other people saw me they wanted to book me for their service too.

I was never in the in-crowd at secondary school, Dixon's City Technology College, although I had a lot of good friends. I often had the mick taken out of me, but I usually just left it, I didn't stand up to it. I wasn't ever bullied really, but I have had fights. I only ever hit someone hard once, but it was hard.

to get our stuff out and the lad and his friends followed us. My locker was by the floor and I felt this guy hitting my back.

I did nothing, but I could feel the rage bubbling inside me. I stood up and he pushed me one more time, so I turned round and punched him ... and he fell, splat! Right on to the floor.

After that I thought, "What have I done?" In only a few seconds his eye started swelling up, you could literally see it rising. I thought I'd better leave.

It takes a lot to get me wound up. I'm not the fighting type, but when I'm angry I really want to lash out. I can usually restrain myself though, that's the only major fight

'I turned round and punched him ... and he fell, splat!'

We were in the science class and I was having a stupid argument with a lad who was trying to pick on me because of my stammer. He was getting at me all through the lesson, which was the last one of the day. When it finished, I stood up to go, the teacher left the classroom but this lad and his mates set on me. "Come on then! Let's have this out!" they shouted. They wanted a fight.

I told them I wouldn't have a fight in school.

"You wimp," said this big lad and he started pushing me about. There was no way I was getting involved, so I backed away calmly but he started to take the mick out of me again. I started to get angry.

"Hold it, Gareth," I thought to myself. "It isn't worth it."

Me and my mates went to our lockers

I've had. My sister was always very good at defending me, she's so protective she'd get into arguments with people over me. I've been lucky to have her around.

I wanted to get into opera as a child, because that's what I'd trained for. I had started to go for auditions, some of them for boybands, because I was starting to really get into pop music – Backstreet Boys, 'NSync, Westlife. When my voice broke, I stopped singing songs from the musicals as my voice was suited to pop stuff, so the interest started from there.

I went to a boyband audition once. The first round was based on looks entirely, and I passed that round. In the next round I had to sing, so that was cool, and I got through. The third round was dancing ... oh no. They seemed to be looking for lads

'If I didn't have that gut feeling I wouldn't be where I am now'

who were more dancers than singers. They didn't want to let me go because of my looks and my voice, but I was really struggling with my dancing, I couldn't remember the routine, so I did a bit of finger clicking (!) and I didn't get through. I'm quite pleased that I didn't now, though!

I thought that perhaps I should leave it and be an opera singer, not a pop star, but my idol was less Pavarotti and more Robbie Williams. Since I was twelve, I'd been working towards getting a place at one of the best music colleges in the world, the Royal Northern School of Music in Manchester. I'd done the audition for the college and the Principal said that he wanted me there. The only thing was that I'd just got a place in the **Pop Idol** auditions in Manchester.

I'd seen an advert on TV about the programme, which told would-be applicants to go online and download the application form. I looked at the website and saw that there was a week or so till the closing date so I knew I had time. A week and a half later I remembered about it, went on the website again and the closing date was, of course ... Saturday morning! It was 11.30 on the Thursday night but I was determined I'd get the form in somehow, so I down-loaded it and printed two out, one for me and one for my sister. I filled in all my details. By this time it was midnight. I went to my sister's bedroom: "Nic! Nic! You've got to wake up and fill this in!"

"Leave it," she said, "it doesn't matter!" I stormed into her room and she pulled the covers over her head.

"Honestly, Nicola, you have to do it," I said. I knew at least I had to do it – I just had this feeling about it.

She eventually got up and filled in her form. Meanwhile I went to my parents' bedroom and knocked on the door.

"Mum! Can you drive us to Asda?" There was a photo booth by the store. "Me and Nic have to have our photos done. Honestly, we have to do it."

My mum immediately got up. She was used to this sort of behaviour – my parents often cut short our family holiday so either Nic or I could do concerts or auditions.

My sister still wasn't too happy about it. "I can't believe you're doing this," she said to me, yawning. "We probably won't get anywhere."

We went over to Asda at about one o'clock in the morning. In the photos I'm smiling from ear to ear and my sister can hardly open her eyes, she's so sleepy.

We sent the application forms Special Delivery so that they were guaranteed to arrive the next day. I was so relieved, because I really thought I had to enter the competition, I don't know why. If I didn't have that gut feeling, I wouldn't be where I am now.

A few months before the first **Pop Idol** audition, I'd started writing songs on the piano and guitar, and although I say it myself, they were quite good! I'd started

'My life was **changing ...**'

taking piano lessons about two years before and got on very quickly – I'm now studying grade six piano.

One of the songs I wrote was a duet for me and my sister, which is wicked, called "From Now To Eternity". The lyrics weren't amazing but they made sense "I'll never forget that night / My darkness turned to light / Your smile I could not hide / The feelings I had inside." That was my verse, then the chorus was, "And our love will last forever / And it was surely meant to be / Promise me (Promise me) / From now till eternity."

Nicola and I have been singing duets together for the last couple of years. Our voices complement each other; I hope to record a duet with her. To have a song in the charts with Nicola would be a dream come true. A brother and sister duet! That would be something different for the charts.

The family cut short another holiday so that my sister and me could go to the **Pop Idol** auditions. She had an audition on Monday, I had one on Tuesday – it was only on Friday that they were filming the auditions with the judges. We were filmed outside the venue singing "Beauty and the Beast" together. We had no idea what to expect when we got in there but we both focused on what we were going to sing.

My sister didn't get through to London, although the judges liked her voice. She went in before me and told me all about it so I knew what to expect. It took ages before it was my turn to go in, but I did and I gave it my best shot. I was made up when I got through and Nic was happy for me too. The Royal Northern was going to have to

wait for me; I couldn't miss this opportunity. I went down to London to go for the next round of auditions, which were at the Criterion Theatre in the West End.

During two days, one hundred contestants were whittled down to fifty; it was quite awe-inspiring to see so many people, who wanted to perform for a living. I was quite quiet, taking it all in. I made a few friends, a girl called Amy who didn't get through and Joanne who was in the final fifty.

Darius was at these auditions, he was like a star to some people because he'd been on **Popstars**. It was the first time I'd met him and he took a shine to me – we played guitar together when we were sitting around the theatre, we played Extreme's "More Than Words" and everyone sang along. We all went out on the last night and I chatted to Darius a lot and got to know him a bit then.

I got into the final fifty and went down to London again as I was in the first group of ten. By now the show had been on TV and I'd been featured quite a bit, I presumed because of my stammer. I thought that they were showing me because I had a good voice, but to say to the audience, "Look! We even get guys who can't talk who want to become a pop star!" I really thought that they wanted the full package; personality plays such a big part in pop music and mine hadn't come out then.

It was a shock when I got to the first group out of the fifty and sat down in the green room before singing rehearsals. Some other contestants presumed I would

get a lot of votes because I'd been featured on the show more than they had. That put a lot more pressure on me to live up to what they were saying, because I didn't see myself as a runaway winner at all. I met Zoë for the first time – I'd not spoken to her much before that and we really bonded. We're both from the north and around the same age. She's amazing, Zoë, she has such a fantastic voice. I was singing "Flying Without Wings" on the show, and I practised with vocal coaches David and Carrie Grant to make sure my performance was the best it could be. I didn't want to mess up this opportunity.

On the following Saturday night, I sang the song as best I could and the audience started voting as the show closed. I was tense then, I had no idea how the votes would go. When something is left to the public vote you know that you could never attempt to predict the result ... it really is the nation's choice. The results came in and ... Zoë and I were through to the final ten! I had 62% of the vote, which was incredible.

"I'm overwhelmed," I said, on live TV – I really was. I went back to school in Bradford and it was manic, everyone wanted to talk to me and some people I didn't count as friends were being nice to me. This was my first taste of what fame would be like. I couldn't go out anywhere without being mobbed.

I was doing my A levels at the time – art, English language and music. I had to leave school in December, when it got to the final ten – we all had to move to London. First I had to give up my place at the Royal College, now my A levels, my life was changing ... something was leading me towards another path.

We had a great laugh during those nine weeks when we all had to sing live every Saturday. Put up in a hotel in west London, we'd work really hard all day rehearsing our songs and filming, then we'd have an excellent time at night, everyone staying up late in each other's rooms, having parties. I spent a fortune on room service ordering food; the bill would come and I'd say, "Whaaat?"

My mum used to ring me every night to check I was OK, so I had to be in my room when she called. When I'd been out, having a party with the others in someone else's room, she'd be annoyed and tell me to go to bed on time. She was only thinking of me, but I wanted to stay up with the others, so I worked it out that I should invite everyone else to my room.

She'd ring and I'd have to tell everyone to be quiet.

I used to answer the phone with an especially weary, "Hello," to sound like I'd just woken up. "What time is it?"

"You in bed, son?" she'd say. "Good."

Then I'd go back to partying.

I loved my time on **Pop Idol**, it was exciting, and everyone was so lovely. I didn't even mind the judges – they always gave constructive comments. I always followed their advice because I thought what they said was accurate. Every week we all had such a laugh, rehearsing and messing around too, but when it came to Saturday and the results show – that was

the worst. I hated that part, the contestants with the lowest vote that week had to sit on a couch, writhing with nerves and it was awful watching them. That was the moment that I got nervous. The evening Zoë went out of the competition was dreadful, I ran up to her and hugged her and I couldn't help but cry. Because we'd met in week one of the final fifty, we stuck together all the time. I was so gutted that night.

The bad thing was that, from the beginning, certain people were saying that I was going to win **Pop Idol**, and I didn't like it at all. I don't think it helped me in any way, it made me self-conscious and I wondered if people would vote against me deliberately, so they felt they had control over what they saw as an inevitable outcome.

The weeks went by and I wasn't voted out. After the first three weeks or so it became a breeze for all of us. We just didn't take in the fact that we were singing live every week to the majority of the UK. The big band night was one of my favourites, because I got to sing "Mack

The Knife" which is a great song, and I think showed a different side to my personality ... because it had an edge to it. I was especially proud of my "biting" mime I did when I sang, "Oh the shark bites, with such teeth, dear ..." Everyone loved it.

The weeks flew by and suddenly, it seemed, it was the night of the final and I was up against Will, who was now a really close friend. I was calm, relaxed even, because I'd been through so much and I knew it was nearly over. The only thing I hated was standing on stage as Ant and Dec announced the result. This time, I was nervous, I had no idea how the voting would go and I wanted to win ... I'd sung my heart out that night, singing "Unchained Melody" especially for my mum.

Will and I got over four million votes each that night, but he just pipped me to the post.

I was genuinely happy for Will, I was made up for him; he has a fantastic voice, so unique. In truth, we were both relaxed during that final night as he and I had been told we'd both get a deal. The night we went to support S Club 7 on the first date of their tour in Dublin, Nicki Chapman sat us down individually and told us that she'd love us to sign to 19 Management and BMG Records. YES! That's when we were assured we'd both succeeded in fulfilling our dream.

Even knowing the result – that I came second – if I could turn back the clock, I wouldn't change a thing. I miss some of the others, but the people I care for I do see quite a bit: Zoë, Will, Rosie and Hayley. I still see members of the production team on other shows. We all got along during the programme, there was a really good

atmosphere about it all. It was a great experience, and it's one of the best things I've ever been involved in. Sometimes I wish I could go back there, to the weeks of the final ten. But now I've got other things to do.'

A WORD FROM PAUL GATES, GARETH'S DAD

'I've always said to Gareth, work hard and you'll be rewarded, that's why I think he's done so well. He's got where he is now due to a combination of very supportive parents, good tuition, a real talent for music and being someone who'll sacrifice things to improve his talents. As a child he gave up a lot of leisure time to concentrate on music, and he gave up playing football, which he was very good at. He's always listened to guidance from us and other people, and takes on board any good advice he's given. He's always wanted to succeed in music, he knows that things aren't just handed to people on a plate. We're immensely proud of everything he's done.'

THE STORY BEHIND …
'UNCHAINED MELODY'
Chapter 2

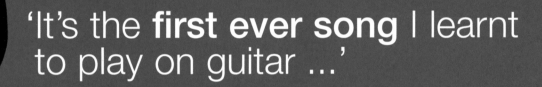

'It's the **first ever song** I learnt to play on guitar ...'

"Unchained Melody" was number one for four weeks from 24 March 2002. It sold over a million and a half copies, going double platinum. Gareth keeps the platinum disc on the floor in his London flat; he hasn't managed to hang it on the wall yet!

'People knew the song from **Pop Idol**, because I sang it when we chose our own songs in the final ten and then I sang it at the final. The reason why I chose it is because it's my mum's all-time favourite song, so I sang it for her. It's great that it was my first single and that it sold so well. I would practise that song over and over again. I learned all the classical stuff in guitar lessons but "Unchained Melody" was the first ever song I learnt to play and

sing at the same time. I used to sit on the doorstep where we lived when I was about eleven with my mates. One of the girls turned round to me and said, "One day you're going to be famous." It means so much to me that it was the first song I could play. The song is on the soundtrack to the film **Ghost**, and that was the first ever film that I ever cried to! How sad!

I'd heard the Robson and Jerome version, but the vocal that I did was taken from the original Righteous Brothers version, which I knew. I know that I wouldn't have been able to make it as good as their version – it's so amazing – so soulful – but I knew I could sing it well.

Once I had chosen the song, Simon Cowell told me that it was also his all-time favourite song! It was lucky for me in a way,

I suppose, but at the same time it made me more nervous; it really put the pressure on. It's a song you can sing very badly. There's a very high note: "I neeeed your love" towards the end, and there are lots of notes you should hold for a quite long time. The Robson and Jerome version is really straight, it's all sung on the beat. In general I like to pull a song around more, so it's not so strictly in time. It's all about phrasing – I don't want to sound all arty but there's an Italian term you learn in music theory which is **rubato**. The literal translation is "robbed time". It's about making the melody more elastic over the song. There's no point trying to change a classic song too much, it's unnecessary, but I made small changes to show that I could make it my own song and that I wasn't trying to copy someone else.

At the rehearsals, I introduced the song by singing, "I'm going to sing this for my mum." I would have said it, but it's much easier for me to sing sentences sometimes, because of my stammer. I had plenty of time in rehearsals but when it came to the live show I felt I had to say it. I tried and I was struggling, then halfway through I thought, "Sack this!" and I started to sing, "And this next song …" Then the intro to "Unchained Melody" came in and I thought, "No!" The song starts almost straight away, so I was halfway through singing my dedication and I missed the line "Lonely rivers flow" and started on "To the sea, to the sea …" Thankfully, I got through the song and didn't let that missed start put me off.

All the judges said I handled it really well, and still put the meaning into it. I was pleased, but I was also thinking, "Oh great! You started without me!"

The response I got from the audience on the night was amazing, and my mum was so proud that she cried – which is the reason why the judges chose it for me to do in the final as well.

The only thing I was still nervous about was making my mum even prouder than when I'd sung it the first time. When I sang it that second time it was even better, I thought – no missed start. I was really pleased.

"That's going to be a number one single for you," Simon Cowell said. I was over the moon. You can't argue with that. It was the obvious choice for a single and it was a big track, absolutely massive!

The song was recorded the day after the final, on the Sunday. Will and I had both recorded "Evergreen" and "Anything Is Possible" a week and a half before, so that whoever won the final could release a single straight away.

I was exhausted, I had suddenly developed a cold, overnight … I'd been fine until the very moment the final ended and then it was as though my immune system

'I had suddenly developed a cold, overnight … **Oh no!**'

had given up and I was ill the next morning.

This wasn't the best day to be sniffling and sneezing. I went into Steve Mac's studio to record the track and I wasn't able to give it my all because I felt so bad. I did a guide vocal, which is a rough recording of the melody line sung over the backing track which people use for timing to sing over, but I couldn't sing it as well as I wanted. The worst thing was that I was going

'Now it felt like I was "Gareth Gates – **pop star**"'

to Florida the very next day, Monday, to film the video, and I had to have a finished track so I could lip sync to it! Oh no! In the end we left the guide vocal on it, and so I had something that I could follow in the video; we were going to record the real vocal when I came back from the video shoot.

I went back into the studio again in a week and tried to follow the guide vocal as much as I could, but it was hard because I was coming up with new ideas which sounded good and I didn't want to ruin the video, which obviously had me singing along to the first recording. In the end me and Steve Mac agreed that the most important thing was the track, not the video, so we did what we wanted to do to make the record even better. The video was just edited not to show shots of me singing where the song had changed.

I had never been to America before and I was really excited, even though I had this awful cold. We were in Tampa, Florida, which is a place where they have a lot of business conferences, but there's a good place called Ybor City, which was originally set up by a guy from Cuba, and has a real New Orleans feel. We didn't go to New Orleans because it would have been more of a nightmare to film – everyone wants to film there, and this place looked amazing, you didn't think you were in Florida at all.

I didn't see a lot of it for the first two days, because I was ill in my bed. The plan was to go to Disneyland but I just wasn't feeling well enough. The shoot took place on the third day, and it was a night shoot, so we started at 5.30 p.m. and didn't finish till 7.30 in the morning. On the street where we were filming, there were loads of clubs, and people were coming out at 2.30 a.m. completely drunk and dancing along with the extras, who were local children with customised cars and the local Harley Davidson drivers' team. If you look closely at the video you can see them all. This week was the first time I felt like a pop star, all the streets were blocked off by the police, it was so cool. Even on **Pop Idol** we were always saying that we didn't feel famous, especially because none of us had had a record out. But now it felt like I was "Gareth Gates – pop star".

I went out a couple of times in Tampa. I went to the aquarium, which I thought would be full of enormous sharks and things, as it's in Florida, but it just seemed to be tiny fish swimming around. I went on a simulator, which again I thought would have an "under the sea" theme with dolphins jumping up out of the water and sharks racing for you in the aquarium. I went in and it was a racing car on the track! I still had my cold at this point so I wasn't feeling great; this simulator was pushing everyone around so badly that I felt much worse when I got off it.

Then I went on a boat ride, which was not what I expected either. I thought it was going to be pleasant, to be able to see dolphins in the water, in a natural environment. The guide on the boat ride spoke into her microphone during the trip: "If you look to the right, you'll see the Tampa chemical plant ..." It was not the best journey!

In the middle of the journey a man came up to us. He was a newspaper journalist, and he wanted to ask some questions. I really felt like a pop star because I was in America – and I've never released a record over there, no one knows me – and I was still being hassled! I quite enjoyed it.

Back in Britain, I realised I had an army of fans who were going wild whenever they saw me. I performed on **CD:UK** and when I hit the high note – "I neeed your love" – everyone started cheering. It was brilliant. Wherever I went, the reaction to that song was massive, because everyone knew it, and would sing along. It was also as if they'd seen me on the TV show for weeks and weeks and now ... I was finally there in front of them, a pop star for real. That made everything more exciting, for me and the fans – the realisation of a dream come true.

Some of the gigs I've done have been unbelievable, the reaction I get – girls screaming and crying when I sing. When I sing "Unchained Melody" I really put my all into it, and perhaps people can feel it. The song means so much to me.

I had an idea the song was going to number one on the first day of release, 18 March 2002. I knew the record shops had ordered a lot of copies, which is a good sign, but you never know until the actual day, you can never take it for granted that it's going to sell.

I loved the cover of the CD: me, Will

and Darius all went to have the shots taken in the week of the final three. The night before the shoot was the night we went to Dublin to do the S Club 7 concert and after that show we went out ... it was a big night. On the morning everyone felt so rough, and the photographer used the strongest light on us which looks great on the pictures but was a bit difficult for us at the time. It worked, though. I used the picture from that shoot just because it was so moody, I loved it.

I was on the **Pop Idol** tour the day "Unchained Melody" was released, and on the Tuesday I spoke to Simon Fuller who told me I'd sold about 300,000 that day, which is loads, especially considering it was chucking it down with rain that day. Monday and Saturday are the two biggest sales days and it rained on both of them. The record did really well; that week it sold almost a million.

On Sunday I was in Birmingham on the **Pop Idol** tour and at 7 p.m. I was sat in a room backstage, holding a little radio in my hand, next to my mum. We had to hear the charts: "At number one, it's Gareth Gates!" Arrgh! It felt so exhilarating, I was so happy, I almost cried.

When it happened it was as if I'd fulfilled every dream of mine. Just before I released the single, people would say, "Gareth, you've made it now," but I knew I hadn't till I had a number one single.

That first week I was at number one was unbelievable, I was so happy. Then, for it to stay at number one for four weeks – incredible. I released the record a month and a half after the show, and I thought that the people that watched the show might not be interested in it at all ... I would never have let any of this go to my head.

I told myself, "Well done", and carried on working hard.

I'm now in the Guinness Book of Records **as the youngest male artist to get to number one in the UK. I've got the framed cover, but I haven't put it on the wall yet. I've had some other things to keep me occupied ...'**

'I had an idea it was going to go to **number one**'

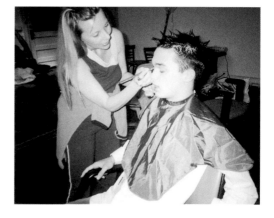

FAME,
OTHERWISE KNOWN AS
GARETHMANIA
Chapter 3

'Gareth! Gareth! **Gareth!**'

Before Gareth Gates enters a room, everyone talks about him. In the weeks it takes to put this book together, he is promoting his new single 'Anyone Of Us'. At a magazine photoshoot in London, people are asking, 'What is he like?' 'Is he quite quiet?' 'Does he still have his stammer?' 'Is he all right? Nice bloke?'

When Gareth does arrive he is chirpy and chatty: one thing you can say about him is that he's not the shy and retiring type. The main thing that comes across is that he is at ease with everything and that nothing seems to trouble him. He is friendly to everyone and talks to the photographer about what he wants for the shoot, then sits down to get his hair done by Ben, his hairdresser, in his beloved '2–2–1' style. He has a slice of toast and looks at the clothes the stylist has bought for the shoot.

He looks like a pop star because he has a lot of confidence, there's something about him, which a few young ladies might have picked up on …

'The sun was shining and the screams were deafening. I'd just played a packed-out Party in the Park in Brighton and the audience had been fantastic. I got out of the car to sign some autographs at the backstage exit. As soon as my spiky hair peeped out of the car door, all the girls started screaming. There were police everywhere, a mad rush, then loads more people started to run up to me. There was a big steel fence and people were being pushed against it and it started getting dangerous.

It was a hot day, girls had taken their tops off so they were just in their bras, asking me to sign their chests.

Everyone's calling my name, "Gareth!

Gareth! Gareth!" It was manic. After a few minutes, the police told us we had to leave because it was too risky, people might get hurt. Everyone was still rushing round the corner from the concert as they've heard I'm at the gates and I had to get back in the car and leave.

In the car, we were surrounded by girls, the traffic was in gridlock so we weren't moving and the girls were banging on the windows and trying to peer in. I think they actually recognise the number plate of the car now, because even though it has blacked-out windows, the girls start staring, they know it's me and start running towards it. I really do worry because they could get hurt.

I did a photoshoot next, still in Brighton, and afterwards I was out on the street, playing football with the chefs who worked in the studio. It was great; I really felt at home then, just having a kickabout, but people started noticing so we drove back to London. That's one thing I miss: not being able to go out as much.

The first time I was recognised from **Pop Idol** was the very night of the first programme, where I was shown at my very first audition for the competition. I was out, celebrating my auntie's birthday in Manchester, and a girl came up to me and said, "Were you on TV tonight?" From then on more and more people knew who I was, until the week of the final ten and it was impossible to go anywhere without being mobbed.

If I go out in a really crowded place then I get instantly recognised, even if I wear a hat – my hair's so obviously me that even if I think I can cover it up, it doesn't work. Sometimes, even if I wear sunglasses, I still get spotted, especially if it's raining, because then I'm drawing more attention to myself ... oh well.

The last time I went out properly was the weekend before the final ten of **Pop Idol**, in Bradford. I was out with my friends Jonathan, Heather, Elan, Claire, Robert and my sister Nicola. We had a real laugh, dancing around the streets and stuff.

'Yes, I met Rachel from S Club...'

I had a feeling that I wouldn't be able to do this ever again, that this was the last time I could mess around in public and that everything would change from there. Now I know I won't be able to do that for a long time, just go out to a normal place without being mobbed, but I do think you have to make sacrifices as a pop star. I always dreamt about being famous and you give up some of your freedom but there are more positives to it than negatives. One positive was when I had to audition some girls for a shoot I did with **Cosmo Girl**. The photos were shot around the sights of London, with me surrounded by these girls. Out of hundreds that turned up I had to pick six, and they were all really good looking, so that was really good fun. Not a bad way to spend the afternoon.'

Wherever Gareth goes, people look at him as if they know him, then realise who he is. Some stare, some mutter, some shriek and run over to him. A lot of women want 'an autograph for my daughter', but you're never sure if it's really for them or not ... From a photoshoot in the morning, Gareth goes for a rehearsal for **SM:TV: Live** at the London Studios. As he gets in the car, a group of thirty schoolgirls passes by. They're on a day trip studying London history, and one of them spots him and they all start whispering to each other ... He's now safely in the car as it drives off slowly, leaving thirty girls, eyes wide almost with disbelief. They've got something extra to put in their project: 'Today we went to see the **Cutty Sark**, remains of the London Wall and pop star Gareth Gates, who I feel I should concentrate on in this essay ...'

Gareth loves the girls: he beams with pleasure that he's been recognised, he seems genuinely happy to be a pop star, and comfortable with it.

'I've met a few famous people, including George Michael who I met the other day, which was wicked. He was working in the same studio as me, and he was really chuffed to meet me ... ha ha! Only kidding. I was the one who was in awe, "It's George Michael!" He's a massive

star. He said well done for all my success, and wished me all the best in the future. He was very nice, considering that I'd beaten him to number one when his single "Freeek!" came out on the same day as "Unchained Melody". It was true what the papers reported, that he sent me a bottle of champagne. He asked me if I'd got it, and I said yes, it's still at 19 Management's office.

I couldn't believe I was standing there talking to him. And I met Sting! I almost forgot! I met him at the Pride of Britain awards, there were hundreds of stars there. The one person I'd love to meet is Michael Jackson – I am such a big fan, but I wouldn't want to meet him until I am a huge star, so I could be on his level and not this guy he's never heard of.

Yes, I met Rachel from S Club. At the time, it was really good, I had such a big crush on her, but I have to say that – honestly – I am so over her now. I have still got the calendar of her and the band, but I've moved on. And now she's engaged, so I wish her the very best!

One of the best moments of this year, when I really thought I'd made it, was singing with Westlife at Earl's Court at the beginning of June. When we were at Pete Waterman's studio during **Pop Idol**, I'd mentioned that my ambition was to sing with Westlife, in front of the cameras in case they were watching, and they invited me on their show. It was a dream come true, and I can't thank the lads enough for making that happen.

Westlife sang the first verse and the chorus of "My Love" and I was on a platform which lifted up from below the stage. I was excited; this was the biggest gig I'd ever played. As soon as I made my appearance, the whole place screamed, it was incredible, ear-splitting. I went into the second verse of the song and I could hardly hear myself. It was amazing, I almost felt like crying. Back offstage and the adrenalin was pumping and I was on a complete high … it was fantastic.

I had met the lads about a week before –

it was Mark's birthday, so I went out with them which was good and a lot of fun. I liked them a lot, especially because they said they loved my version of "Flying Without Wings" – they all said they voted for me. Well, there would have been trouble if they hadn't ...'

Gareth has to stop off from the **SM:TV: Live** rehearsal to go shopping, because it's Father's Day on Sunday and he hasn't got his dad a present yet. He wanders round one of the big, swanky department stores looking at the wallets, deciding which one his dad might like. After a lot of pondering he gets interrupted by some Japanese fans, who take a photo of themselves with Gareth, are extremely polite and leave quickly. After a bit more pondering, he plumps for a very nice brown leather wallet, pays for it, then goes down to get it gift-wrapped so it looks even more special. Young girls, dragged along by their parents, stop when they see him, mouths open, not believing their eyes. As Gareth passes the card department he has to stop and buy a card for his dad, then he spots a card a friend might like, then another ... soon he's got more cards in his hands than occasions to celebrate and the more he's hanging around the more he's being recognised ... there's no problem when one person spots him, but when twenty people do, they all stop and stare, and that attracts thirty more people who want to see what the commotion is about ... which then attracts more and more ...

'I went to LA to shoot the cover for "Anyone Of Us" and take more shots for the album. I thought I'd have no problem in LA because I'm not known over there, so we could get on nice and quietly with the shoot and not get hassled. I got out of LAX airport and all was calm, but all of a sudden there was a flashbulb in my eyes and then we were surrounded by photographers.

What happened was that people back here knew I was going over there so they'd tipped off some people. I tried to keep my head down but, to be honest, I thought it was great! Everyone was shouting, asking some really funny questions, like, "What do I think of world peace?" "Yeah, it's good," you could say, but it's best not to answer those sorts of things at all!

Some photographers decided to chase us in our car and we had to escape – it was mental, they were all over the road, they almost caused some really bad accidents. They were trying to tail us because they wanted to know where my hotel was. It was a bit hairy, but on the way we were able to lose them, which was really funny because it was just like a film – the fact that you're in America makes it more cinematic.

I enjoyed it loads, especially as I'd never been to LA before and it looks so different from anywhere else.

When you're on the streets and having your photo taken in different places you look the part, so everyone's thinking, who's he? That was good. Some bloke came up to me on Hollywood Boulevard, he looked a bit like a middle-aged Elvis, but scruffy. He was joking around, telling me who he was and how I should clear off the Boulevard because he was so famous. He asked who I was and I said I was a number one singer from Britain and he suddenly backed off. It was funny – some British tourists spotted me in LA too, they knew me so I really couldn't escape ... We had such a laugh doing the shoot, in LA and in the desert ... the whole team was in hysterics most of the time because we kept seeing these signs for "jerk" food

which they have over there, so its was "jerky" this and "jerk" that, so I got as many pictures as I could of me standing by the signs. I was in stitches the whole time.

In Britain I hide myself away a bit, or only go to restaurants where they're used to having famous people there. If they're not, they're straight on the phone to the press – I understand that because it's publicity for the restaurant, but it means you can't go anywhere without being watched. Still, there are worse things for an eighteen-year-old to deal with, so I'm not complaining.'

Gareth has an interview and photoshoot at Home House, a posh hotel in which he first stayed when he moved down to London. He is nostalgic, 'Do you think they'll let me see my old room?' he asks. 'I had so much fun here.' He orders Pepsi and a steak and chips, but is wary of the béarnaise sauce as he worries it might have cheese in it, which could set off a migraine. He talks about a time when he tried, but failed, to get on the roof of the hotel, which is dome-shaped, because he wanted to lie down on the dome 'for a laugh'. The fact that if he had done so he might have crashed through the ancient glass, hurtled down past the staircase and landed (or splatted) a hundred feet below doesn't seem to have crossed his mind. He is without much self-consciousness, he breezes through each day, as busy and demanding as it is.

When the interviewer he is speaking to today accidentally spills water on his mobile phone when she gets up to leave, he is all smiles and tells her not to worry. When she's gone, he studies his phone, checking it's all right, but says nothing more. Gareth is a natural charmer.

'Now that I'm famous, I don't feel like

'Some photographers decided to **chase us** in our car and **we had to escape ...** '

a different person, I'm just in a different situation, but I love it. To go from being an everyday child, then all of a sudden if you walk down the street everyone's screaming at you, was strange, but I am getting used to it now. I have to admit that I love the attention from girls, I'll always try and stay a while and chat. Some girls will try to tear my clothes off, they try to rip my jacket or my shirt. I'm sure they'd pull off my arms if they could but I wouldn't change that for anything.

I get loads of fan mail and I get some strange requests: people ask me to marry them and they ask me to have their babies, it can be a bit saucy. I get knickers sent to me through the post and on the stage I get thrown knickers, thongs. I find it funny.

"Garethmania" is growing, it gets more intense as the weeks go by, I can feel it. It's only in this country, I haven't yet released a record in Europe, and when I do I hope it will go mental. I've got Asia and America to do as well, and my main aim is to break America. I want to be happy, that's important, and the minute I'm not I'll stop what I'm doing. I believe if you're in something you should enjoy it and if you don't then you shouldn't be in it. There are thousands who would like to be where I am now. I've wanted this for so long and wanted it so badly that I could never be complacent.

I don't want to become arrogant either, but you have to know that there's a reason you were chosen out of the thousands that applied: that you must be good. But there's a fine line between being confident in yourself and being over-confident and arrogant. You have to believe in yourself but you have to understand where you're from. I know that my sister Nicola would be the first to tell me

if I was stepping out of line she'd hit me.'

Gareth rushes back to his flat in west London, which is so secure and out of the way, surrounded by fences, that you could mistake it for a fortress. It has to be this way – he's tried walking around the local area but any more than five minutes and there's a stampede. For now, Gareth is happy and wouldn't change anything.

'I'm a pop star, and that's what you have to expect.'

'"Garethmania" is **growing ...**'

MY **SPEECH PROBLEM**
AND **THE McGUIRE PROGRAMME**
Chapter 4

'In my German GCSE oral exam I actually had to **sing my answers out ...**'

'I was never able to truly express myself until I started learning the guitar. All of a sudden I had found an instrument that could "speak" for me and I found I could get everything out of me through music. If you look at it a certain way, having a stammer has really helped me musically, because it was such a release. I needed it. Obviously I didn't choose to have a stammer, but if I'd been without music I'd be some person who is very much held back ... Actually, I don't know what I'd be without it. People say, "Music is my life" or "Sport is my life", but I know it's my life, music is me, it helps me communicate.

Not everyone who has a stammer can channel it like me. I know I'm lucky to have a talent, and because of that I've never been introverted. Whenever it was the first term at a new school for me, my mum would go marching to see the head of the school and explain that I had a bad stammer so they would understand. Every time she'd be told, "But Mrs Gates, Gareth seems to have no problems integrating at all. He's doing extremely well already."

Some people, before they meet me, expect me to be shy, but I'm outgoing most of the time.

My stammer got progressively worse through school. In my German GCSE oral exam, I actually had to sing my answers out because I couldn't speak. I was finding it so hard to say anything at all that my "Ich bin Gareth" turned into a sort of rap and the teacher just had to laugh. I did all right though, I got an A – overall I got seven A grades in my GCSEs.

When I was doing my A levels I heard about the McGuire programme, and I wanted to try it. It was only coincidence that I went on the course just after the first round of **Pop Idol** auditions; I'd been booked to do it for months as I was just at an age when I wanted to control my speech.

The first course I took was in Liverpool over four days; it was for beginners and people who'd done the course before. The course was constructed by Dave McGuire, who was a stammerer. He was frustrated with the methods he had already come across, so he wanted to use old techniques and apply new ones to find something new. The people helping out on the course were all recovering stammerers, and the emphasis was placed on therapy but also support. That's where I met Michael Hay, amongst others, who has given me a lot of help, especially after the course when he was at the other end of the telephone.

This programme was absolutely fantastic for me, it really does work, although it doesn't advertise itself as a "cure". I was determined that I should work on my speech when I went there, I didn't want to mess around. "I'm going to go for it," I thought. I could sing to a cathedral full of people but I still couldn't speak.

The first day I was at the course in Liverpool, everyone in our group had to sit in a chair, with a video camera in front of us, and someone would ask us our name, where we were from, and many other questions. I was so nervous and I was at my worst then and I struggled like mad – speaking in front of eight strangers was nerve-wracking. Everyone's really quiet, just listening to you, and it took me five minutes to say my name.

The reason why saying your own name is the most difficult thing to say is that it's something that everyone asks you, "Hi! What's your name?" Because you know that you have to say it the first time you're going to meet someone, you think, "Right, I'm going to go for it ..." but all that thinking about it beforehand makes it worse and you can't get it out at all. That in turn makes you worse and worse.

On the first day, Thursday, you do a lot of breathing techniques, making sure you have a smooth flow of air when you speak. By the end of the day it should be much easier to say your name and where you're from. That's the physical aspect.

By Saturday, the programme is working on the psychological aspect. Everyone goes out onto the streets and you ask people for the time, or ask them to show you the way to Marks and Spencer's, everyday things. Then you explain what you're doing, "I'm on a speech programme, and today my target is to speak to over a hundred people", so you naturally have to get into conversation. For a stammerer to do that ... it's so hard. The course places you in situations that you really hate and you have to do them. We also had to make loads of phone calls, which is rock hard, ringing up hotels and asking if you can reserve a room. I hated it but I could see what they were doing, and it was helping me so much.

The last thing you have to do is the real test. On the Saturday afternoon, peak shopping time when the town is packed,

'Some papers claimed my **stammer** was a **hoax**'

you have to stand on a soapbox in the middle of the town and speak. As soon as you're standing on this thing everyone gathers round.

"My name is Gareth Gates!" I shouted, on my soapbox. I was amazed at my progress, on the Thursday morning I couldn't get anything out.

"I am a recovering stammerer. Four days ago I couldn't say my name but now I can."

I said a bit more and I didn't stammer at all: I was so proud of myself, I really was. The programme is the best thing I've done. I did another course in Birmingham for four more days before the final ten of **Pop Idol**, but the funny thing is that I didn't get up on the soapbox this time because people knew who I was already. I'd say, "Hi, my name's ..." and they'd say, "I know your name, it's Gareth Gates," so I couldn't carry on!

The good thing is that everyone understands what you're going through

on the course, the admin, the instructors, everything is run by recovering stammerers. You can see that some people have had a really hard life with it. I felt for them, I haven't ever let it hold me back from fulfilling my dream. One of the messages I wanted to get out to people in the **Pop Idol** show was that even though you have a disability, you shouldn't let it stop from what you want to do. I have met people now who have a stammer, people who can't walk, people who are blind, and some have said to me, "I want to thank you, the courage you had has made me think that I can do what I want." That's great, that makes me happy.

There was a point during **Pop Idol**, just after the second McGuire course, that my speech got a lot better. Some papers claimed my stammer was a hoax. All my life I've struggled and I'd had to put up with people mocking me; for the papers to turn round and say I was faking it … I was really shocked. Why would I want to do that? Why would I make it up? That they could say that surprised me, but I've set the record straight now.

The only problem I've had is not being able to go to support meetings enough to practise the breathing technique. Michael has been wonderful and used to come along to **Pop Idol** and stand in the green room when we had TV interviews. When I was struggling with words I'd look at Michael and be able to speak. Eye contact is very important, if you have nothing to focus on you're distracted and just think about how you're going to get your words out. If you look a person in the eye, you get respect from them, and from that you get self respect.

On the Birmingham course in October 2001 I met George Samios, who has also been a tremendous help. I would like to thank all the people I have met on the McGuire programme. They have all been an inspiration to me, helping me on the road to recovery.'

A WORD FROM MICHAEL HAY

'I started on the programme a year before I met Gareth in Liverpool, and we became good friends from then on. We kept in touch, and I was the main guy Gareth rang for advice. As he mentions, support is the key.

Gareth was one of the strongest people on the course. He's incredibly focused and hard-working – if he wants something he gets it, he doesn't give up. The frustrating thing for him was that he got so busy with Pop Idol and couldn't practise as much, he found that hard.

We all treat it like it's a "sport" of speaking, you have to practise and keep the exercises up to do it. The goal is not fluency, it's about speaking well, carefully choosing the words you want to say; eloquence is the goal. If you think of yourself as a fluent speaker then you put yourself under pressure because you're scared of stammering again. Gareth's really learnt that that's the best way to look at it.'

THE STORY BEHIND ...
'**ANYONE OF US**'
Chapter 5

At the time of writing, 'Anyone of Us' – the song detailing a minor indiscretion and the regret on the part of the singer, longing for his true love – has just come out. Gareth is in the middle of promoting the single, which he's doing every day.

'This was written by the people who wrote "Evergreen" and Britney Spears' "Baby One More Time": Jorgen Elofsson, Per Magnusson and David Kreuger, and was recorded in April 2002. I was excited to go to Sweden to record with them; the songs they've written are amazing. Three of them write but only two of them produce: Per and David. I find them funny because although they know how to speak English, they don't really understand the English sense of humour. I like to have a laugh when I'm there in the studio with them and I try to make a joke, or spot something I think is funny and they're always stony-faced. If I mock myself in some way they don't get it at all, so we just get on with recording!

I love to work with them, because they're the same as me, every word and every line has to be perfect. I've worked with other producers, they say, "That's OK" when I think it has to be the best you can do it. I like people who push me in the studio, it's hard work but the results are obviously thousands of times better.

It does help if the producer has written the song and then produces it, because they know exactly how they want you to sing it and you can be guided; you know then what meaning you're trying to get out of the lyrics. There's always a subtext in the lyrics, the words never have just one level to them, so it's good when someone knows the song inside out. They say things like, "Imagine you're singing to someone, a nice girl." They're very good at knowing what singers can do to produce a different sort of sound, and they're always telling you to use the front of the mouth or lighten the tone a little bit.

They did tell me how to sing specific lines on this song. I sing, "'Cos I made a stupid mistake" at the end of the chorus

'I have been having **posh food** lately...'

and I was singing it like I say it, "stupid". I was in the vocal booth and they kept telling me, "No no no! Sing it like it's 'stoopid'!" I couldn't do it for ages, I kept saying it my way, but in the end I sang "stoopid mistake" and they loved it, they said that's the way it had to be. That's how perfectionist they are.

During this trip to Sweden I went out to a bar and had something to eat, which was quite posh. I find if I go out to expensive places, they're often really quiet, but I'm not a person to change my behaviour because of where I am or who I'm with: I'm me and that's it. So I was having a laugh with Camilla, my PA, we were both being loud and everyone else was really quiet ... it was good fun.

I have been having posh food lately in these sorts of places, so I'm starting to get to know more about restaurant food, and I think it's hilarious. The first time I took my sister out when she was in London she was reading the menu, and she had no idea what anything was: "What's that?" "What's that?"

We just had a laugh with it then: if there was a nice soup on the menu, we'd say to the waiter, "But have you got Heinz soup? Tomato? Oxtail?" They didn't understand it at all; we were killing ourselves laughing.

And when they hand round the bread basket, it's all got this stuff in, nuts and things. We'd say, "Have you got some Hovis?"

They always say, "What's Hovis?"

When I took my sister out another time, we went to a place and the portions were absolutely tiny, and also she wasn't keen on what she had. On the way back we

decided to get McDonald's!

We filmed the video in Venice. Each year around February time they have a carnival, and one event is where everyone

'I think it was a bit more than a **snog**'

wears masks. The video makers, Max and Dania, who made the video for "Unchained Melody", wanted to have that theme, so it would look really colourful and the video storyline would go with the song. The song's describing a person who's cheated on his girlfriend. He's saying that it was only a little thing, that it didn't mean anything to him, hence the words, "She means nothing to me ..."

I think it was a bit more than a snog. The second verse goes, "She must have altered my senses as I offered to walk her home ..." so I think it was very much a "come in for a coffee" situation, you know.

I play the role of this guy who's cheated on his girl, and he goes to a masked ball hoping she's going to be there, but she isn't ... so I'm looking round at all the people, and because they're wearing masks I can't find her. I look all round the city, all through the canal and at the end it's just a shot of me on a boat going off into the distance ... to be continued ...

I had to do a bit of acting in the video, I'm sitting on the edge of a bed and I look like I'm sorry for cheating on my girlfriend in the song. It was easy for me to act, when I sing I put the emotion and expression into the song. Some people don't sing when they lip sync to a video or mime on **Top of the Pops**, but you can tell they're miming because they don't breathe properly. If you're singing as well, you do look like it, you're not just mouthing the words. I always sing along.

I wore a great suit by Hugo Boss made out of cashmere, so it got a bit hot; the tie and the shirt were from Paul Smith, I love that outfit. It was raining a bit in Venice when we filmed, and it was quite smelly because of the sewers. One of the lighting guys fell in the canal when we were on the boat, and he had an awful smell about him all day, poor bloke. We worked for two days on the video, and at nights I'd be so tired I'd go back to my hotel and go to bed. There wasn't much going out for me.'

A WORD FROM THE VIDEO DIRECTOR: DANIA, FROM MAX AND DANIA

'**Gareth was great, he picks things up very quickly and he knows how to turn the charm on. We had one hour in the hotel room for rehearsal and performance and he wasn't put off by the crew at all; he was a very good actor. He's an absolute natural, he shines in front of the camera and he's very comfortable with it all.**'

GIRLS
Chapter 6

'I had a **different girlfriend every week** when I was really young'

Gareth Gates is known for being quite a hit with the ladies. When he's out, girls simply stare at him, it's something he doesn't mind in the slightest. Sitting with Gareth, when the TV is on in the corner, his eyes dart to the set whenever he glimpses a good-looking girl ... He just can't help himself.

'I've always been popular with girls, even before **Pop Idol**, because I used to do shows at school. I was known by all the girls in every class, there's something they like about a singer. Yes, the girls go wild when I perform now, but to be honest they went mad when I was fourteen, just on a smaller scale. I've been singing since I was eight, so I built up a following over time ... One of the shows we did was called **Stars in Their Eyes**, it wasn't like the TV show where you pretend to sing like someone, it was a straightforward talent show. I sang "My Love" by Westlife and "Angels" by Robbie Williams. It's funny because I sang that song with Westlife when I was at Earls Court. If I'd known that then ...

I think that, because of my stammer and because I used to sing a lot, girls found me really approachable and I found that most of my best friends would be girls. I had really good male friends but girls liked me, perhaps because I was less loud than other boys.

'I've **never** fallen in love ...'

I had a girlfriend when I was about five, but I wouldn't want to name her, nor the girl who I had my first kiss with, because I still know her! I haven't spoken to her for years and years but I heard that about a year ago she was asking about me ... She was just really nice, sweet. I'm not saying any more! And anyway, I had a different girlfriend every week when I was really young. When I was at school, the eleven-year-old girls used to stick pictures of me on their diaries.

As well as Bradford Cathedral choir, I was in the school choir. For the first two years, I was the only boy in the choir. It was all girls and I loved it. Now the school choir has far more boys in it, so perhaps I set the precedent. In my A level group and in music I was the only lad as well.

I haven't ever had a proper girlfriend. I've had girlfriends but I haven't had a proper relationship. From the age of twelve, I was going out with girls, to the pictures and stuff. I've even met a few parents, which is the scariest thing about a relation-ship, but nothing's been serious or full time. I seemed to have all these activities to fit seeing girls around ... and I'd get really busy and then it got difficult.

I don't have a type, I haven't got a preference in colour of hair. I once said I liked blondes but really during my early teens I had a crush on a redhead, a brunette, a blonde ... Loads of girls used to ask me out ... I had a couple of months of not eating right or sleeping right because of one girl, who was a friend of my sister. Whenever the phone rang, she picked it up, so I used to sit next to her, to try and hear if she was talking about me ... I had quite strong feelings for her, but it didn't come to anything – I was only young!

The important thing to me about a girl is her personality – the sort of person I am, with my speech, she has to be patient and understand what I'm going through. If it's taking a while for me to get something out, she mustn't shout, "Oh, hurry up!"

Looks are the first thing that catch your eye in a girl, and then you get to know her. If I'm in a room just talking to someone and I look over and there's a beautiful girl there, I'm definitely interested, but I'd have to get to know her a bit first and see if she's a nice person.

The press are fascinated by my private life, which I find funny. They said things about me and Zoë when we were just really good mates and they try to make it into something more. They're really interested in my friendship with Hayley. You read things you don't even know about yourself most of the time.

It's difficult to have a proper girlfriend as a pop star, and I really would love a proper girlfriend. It's unfair on a girl because of my commitment to my music

'There's people wanting a **relationship** with me because of **what I am**, not **who I am**'

and my heavy work schedule: I'm busy every day and that can be difficult for a girl. I can't have a serious relationship – it wouldn't be fair. It's also hard, because girls would get jealous of me being on TV and an idol of other girls. But really, one dream of mine is to have a big house in Yorkshire and a wife and children, that is something that I want ... in a few years.

If the right girl did come along, I'd go for it. I wouldn't say, "I've got to wait a few years." You can't help the way you feel for someone. As I said, I've never fallen in love, but it's not something I'm scared of, I look forward to it, I know it can be the best

thing that ever happens to you ...

I get propositioned by girls all the time, and I see the way some girls act around me now: they get very excited. It's strange, I still think of myself as an everyday guy. Most girls who talk to me are lovely, but a small minority are very forward, and I think, "What are you after?" I'm aware that there's people wanting a relationship with me because of what I am, not who I am. There are lots of girls who see me on TV and hear the records in the charts and that's why they are attracted to me.

The test for any girl will be my sister: even though she's younger, she is very protective of me. She's seen more girls flock around me recently – those I've never met before and those that I used to know and lost contact with. She's very sharp, and I think she can suss out everything very well, she can tell those whose motives aren't genuine. One of her favourite new phrases is, "I know what **she's** after." The fans have got to be scared of my sister, not me. If they pass my sister they're all right.'

THE **ALBUM**
Chapter 7

'People might think that I'm just a pop star who comes into the studio and records a vocal then goes back home again. It's not like that at all'

THEALBUM67

Gareth is still in the middle of writing and recording his debut album with different producers, fitting in sessions between promotion and performances.

'I've just been in the studio with Steve Mac and he's fantastic to work with, I especially asked to work with him. He's worked with Simon Cowell on other projects and we've been working together quite a bit. He's the one who produced "Unchained Melody".

The way that we write together seems to work well because we work in a similar way. I like tracks that have a key change in them, always – "Unchained Melody" didn't, because it was a cover version, but we've written another that has two key changes. It really lifts the song. If you listen out, you hear them in loads of pop songs.

The album is going to have songs, each with a different feel to them: ballads, up-tempo stuff and some smooth little numbers. I've recorded quite a lot but we're not near finishing yet ... I can tell you that I'm pretty sure I've recorded my Christmas single, and it's an amazing song, just fantastic. I'm very excited about it, I really am. The album hasn't got a title, because we haven't finished ... so I'd better hurry up then, hadn't I?

People might think that I'm just a pop star who comes into the studio and records

'I won't be happy with a vocal unless **every note** is **exactly** the way it should be'

a vocal then goes back home again. It's not like that at all. Because I had musical training, I'm fascinated by how different producers write and I like to work with them on my songs. I have loads of input in songwriting.

When I walk into the studio, I sit down with the producer and we decide what sort of song we're going to record, whether it's a ballad, something mid-tempo or a fast song. We then put together a chord structure, and while we're doing that we play around with ideas and vocal melodies. Then we begin to play with words, come up with a theme for the song and try to find the hookline. The end of chorus can be the hookline, like "Make it evergreen" on "Evergreen". Then that becomes the title of the song. "Stupid mistake" is a hookline, however, the title of song is "Anyone Of Us (Stupid Mistake)", so it doesn't always work like that. You can have the hookline at the start of the chorus too, it's whatever makes the song catchy.

I'm learning how to put words together and write lyrics that make sense and sound right when you hear them on a record, which is an art in itself. You don't need to write grammatically correct lyrics, in "Evergreen", there's a line that goes, "You're more beautiful than I have ever seen." That doesn't make strict sense; you wouldn't be able to write that in an English exam, but the meaning comes through.

Writing lyrics is hard. It can take a long time to go through all the possibilities of a story within the song. I do write some autobiographical things, about love and stuff, but I'm only young so I haven't had a huge experience of it.

I play some instruments on a few of the tracks. When I was working with Ray Hedges on a song, I did all the keyboard parts: playing strings and bass on a synthesiser. On other tracks I've done some guitar as well.

Sometimes, when I've met a producer for the first time, they've been really surprised that I can read music, but I know that you don't have to have that skill to write great pop music necessarily. In pop music it's all about experience, not about an in-depth knowledge of it, it's about the right sounds and where they go.

I'm a big fan of Westlife and Backstreet Boys records, amongst others. They have that polished, perfect quality to their records; that's the kind of sound I go for. The sound is full, the harmonies are tight. I won't be happy with a vocal unless every note is exactly the way it should be. Some people say there's more character in the song if it isn't sung perfectly. I see what they mean but if you spend ages singing a line, to get everything out of it, it's so much better than just singing it a couple of times and thinking, "That'll do." It's about quality!

Although I haven't had any vocal coaching since **Pop Idol**, I feel that my singing gets stronger and stronger, just with practise. My voice isn't mature yet, it doesn't finish breaking properly until you're 21, so in three-to-four years' time I will be so much better compared to now –

you see, I never take anything for granted; I'm always aware I could be better.

All this makes the work in the studio quite intense, but I get so into it. It takes me half an hour to warm up and get used to the song and then I sing until I'm happy and the producer's happy. I stay focused on what I'm doing, not let my mind slip ... but it's not too exhausting. I always try to have a laugh in the studio.

At the moment I've been writing some tracks myself. I don't know how many of them will be on the album, but if one or two are on there, I'll be very happy. I'm picking up loads of tips on how to record and produce. It's only really small stuff but I'm working in more and more studios and I'm a quick learner. I'm always watching what everyone's doing. I'm not just sitting there on the sofa reading a magazine.

In the future I want to write and produce my own stuff, but that's a long way ahead and I'm happy with everything the way it is. There's still a lot to learn, I've had a good grounding, for my voice and for instrument playing. As a musician I'm a good all-round person, but I haven't done everything yet, I don't know it all.'

A WORD FROM A RECORD PRODUCER, RAY HEDGES

'I have to say I am very impressed with Gareth: he's a talented musician as well as a good singer. He's reached a high level with piano and guitar and that makes a big difference. His ideas for melody are much stronger than most. He has a different understanding of music; he suggests chords and things and he was intrigued when we showed him some chord progressions he hadn't seen before. He's also really good at lyric ideas. When he came in the studio it was really good, he's a lovely guy, talented, but very modest: he never bragged about his classical training. We try and have a laugh when people come down, but we also work very hard and it was refreshing to work with someone who was prepared to fight until everything was right – he didn't get frustrated ... the one other thing I'd mention is that he really loves his pizza.'

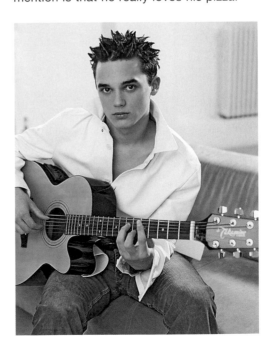

TIME **OFF**
Chapter 8

We got the late train, Mum picked us up from Bradford Station once we were back, at half twelve. She was furious. I'd love to relive that, apart from Mum going mad.

'The last mobile phone bill I got was for £400'

I used to take my Walkman around with me everywhere I went, but now I've got an iPod which you use in conjunction with a Mac computer. You can put everything on it – MP3s, CDs, – it stores up to a thousand songs, so it saves you carrying loads of CDs around with you. Mine is getting a bit scratched because I use it so much. They haven't made a case for it and I wish they would.

When you go away for promotion and tours you get used to living out of a suitcase because you're staying in hotels all the time. I moved down to London after **Pop Idol** and stayed in an amazing place, Home House. I stayed there for so long that I used to call it just "Home" and left the "House" bit out.

When there's nothing else to do and you're on your own, it gets boring being in a hotel room. It was fine during **Pop Idol** and on the tour, I enjoyed all that, but when that was over I got lonely at times ... Obviously, if I've got down-time then I'm on the phone. I've got two phones, one for work, one for friends. The last bill I got was for £400. I spend so much time on the phone because of my speech – I spend ages trying to get the words out – so that's why it's so expensive ...'

THE **FUTURE**
Chapter 9

'They say I'm a role model now, which is great'

'The principal at my last school, Mr John Lewis of Dixon's City Technology College in Bradford, has given me the Principal's Award 2002. Every year he gives out this award for someone who's worked hard and done the school proud. He says he usually finds it difficult to single someone out, but this year it was easy.

It's not because of what I did on **Pop Idol**, it's simply because I was so involved in the music department at school and I'm one of the people he can use as an example of what can come out of the school. I think that they were an example themselves, because they invested a lot of time into me there, and were always supportive of me.

They say I'm a role model now, which is great. I used to work really hard on my school work and for the school to recognise that is really good. I wouldn't be where I am now without having my parents behind me, making sure I did all my work. Of course I used to laze around sometimes and not practise my instruments or get my homework in when it was due, but I was generally very disciplined. I really don't think I would be in this position if I didn't understand that. You don't realise until you look back in retrospect, but you see that if you're brought up to take yourself and your work seriously, then it gives you a good grounding later on.

Will and I are doing a duet for the next single, which I'm looking forward to so much. It will be perfect for the tour that Will and I are doing together. I'm so looking forward to the tour, because I don't see Will

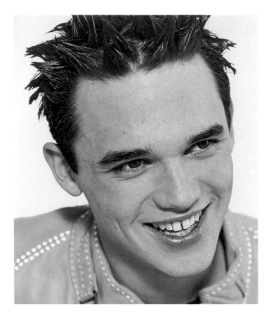
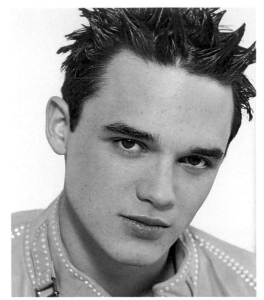

very often and he's a really good friend. A lot of people instantly think that we hate each other, because we were rivals on the final of **Pop Idol**, but we aren't like that at all, we're very close. Hopefully people can see that in the duet. We're very different people, he's older and a bit posher than me, but he's such a nice lad and he's got the best voice, such an amazing voice. On the final of **Pop Idol** everyone was asking me, "Why aren't you really upset you didn't win?" The reason why was because I was so happy for Will. I have loads of respect for him, he had so much courage to come out and tell people that he was gay; he was under loads of pressure.

In the future I'd like a nice big house in Yorkshire, out in the fields. I'll get a place in London but I want to think about my family first. People come up to visit our house in Bradford all the time, it's manic. Girls travel from all over the country just to sit outside for a couple of hours, even when I'm not there. Whenever my family comes down to London to see me, they bring a massive pile of photos for me to sign, so they can

take them back to Bradford. I greet them with my pen in my hand because I expect it now. When I went back to Bradford a month ago, my mum had a party for me. All my aunties and uncles came along, and she invited all my friends from the past and old music teachers – everybody I ever knew was there. It was brilliant. I saw old friends like Lee for the first time in years, and he was the same – although a lot taller now. It was hard because everyone wanted to talk to me, so I couldn't have a long, deep conversation with anyone, but it was really good to catch up with people.

If I am a role model then I want to continue being a role model for people. I want to help people: the hungry, the homeless and the hurting. My faith is important to me, it grounds me. If I'm in a position that I can benefit other people, then I think it's really important that I should do it; I want to be successful in myself but I'm also here so I can help others. I don't want anyone to think I'm only doing it to win people over, it's not like that at all, it's a personal thing.

'I want to help people: the hungry, the homeless and the hurting'

I love what I do, I think I'm so lucky,
and every day gets better and better.
I'd never take it for granted, or moan
about it, because it's amazing. To be
in this position at eighteen is all I could
have ever wanted – and it is something
that I've wanted for so long. If I can do
anything to help others then I will, and
I will be so happy to be able to do that.
Every day I wake up and I'm thankful
for being here. I truly love it.'